Daily Bread

Simple Facts on Diet and Nutrition

Dr Yatish Agarwal

जय विज्ञान JAI VIGYAN
२००४
वैज्ञानिक जागरूकता वर्ष
Year of Scientific Awareness

Rajkamal

Rajkamal Books
1-B Netaji Subhash Marg
Daryaganj, New Delhi – 110 002
Tel: 011-232 74463; 232 88769 *Fax*: 23278144
E-mail: Info@rajkamalprakashan.com

ISBN: 978-81-267-1036-2

First published in the *Year of Scientific Awareness*, 2004

This edition, 2012

Advisors
Dr R.S.K.Sinha, MD
Dr Dinesh Singhal, MD, DM

Editor : Manju Gupta
Creative Director : Abhimanyu Sinha
Graphics : Tapas Sarkar, Naresh Sharma
Production : Mahesh Chandra

The author can be reached on the e-mail at: **dryatish@yahoo.com**

₹ *60*

Printed at B.K. Offset
Shahadra, Delhi-110 032

Contents

The Daily Bread Plan

Eating Right

Eating is not merely for carnal pleasure. It is essential to life. Seated at life's dining table, if you ponder over the virtues of food, you would quickly realize that without it, everything shall come to a grinding halt. From the moment we begin the journey of life, food helps us build, grow, maintain and protect our bodies—giving us sustenance, energizing our brains to think, our hearts to beat, our bodies to dance in step with the melody of life.

One cannot think well, love well, sleep well,
if one has not dined well.

Virginia Woolf
A Room of One's Own

When life originated on this planet, man's plate was full of natural foods. It gave him strength and vigour to sustain life through all odds. Yet, over time, man drew away from the simple conventions of Mother Nature, weaving complexities in his life, and a need arose to define the criterion of a wholesome diet.

Staying healthy: the basic nutrients

The human body needs at least six types of nutrients to foster life. These are:

- Carbohydrates
- Proteins
- Fats
- Vitamins
- Minerals
- Water

Carbohydrates

Carbohydrates are the body's key source of energy. They provide four calories of energy per gram. During digestion, carbohydrates are broken down into simple sugars, the simplest of them being glucose. It is glucose that fuels the billions of cells that make our body.

Depending on the number of components and how they are linked together, a carbohydrate is classified as simple carbohydrate (sugar) or complex carbohydrate (starch). Simple sugars are found in fruits and many vegetables; milk products; and honey, sugarcane and sweets. Common starch foods include whole-grain breads and cereals, beans, peas, potatoes and certain vegetables. The human body breaks down starches during digestion into simple sugars to form glucose.

To help with meal planning, nutritionists classify carbohydrates into four groups:

Vegetables. This group includes all non-starchy vegetables.

Fruits. All fruits, from the ubiquitous apples, bananas and oranges to the exotic alphonso mangoes, kiwis and prickly pears contain the simple sugar, fructose.

Milk products. Milk and milk products contain lactose, a simple sugar.

Starches. Bread, rice, beans and certain vegetables, such as potatoes, and corn, are made up of complex carbohydrates.

Diet *pandits* believe that about half the daily calories should come from carbohydrates. Besides milk, carbohydrates which contain plenty of natural fibre such as grains, fruits, and vegetables are good for health. They offer several benefits: exerting a steadying influence on the blood sugar, limiting the absorption of cholesterol from food, and providing vitamins and minerals. In comparison to processed foods, they are much healthier.

Processed foods contain too much simple sugar, too much fat and are devoid of vitamins and minerals. Since processed foods only provide useless calories, they are referred to as junk foods.

Proteins

The main function of proteins in the body is to build and repair body tissues. They also shape the enzymes that speed up chemical reactions, neurotransmitters that serve as chemical messengers, globulins that fight infection and albumin that regulates the distribution of water in the body. They also form haemoglobin by joining hands with iron to transport oxygen from the lungs to the body's tissues.

Proteins are made of smaller units called amino acids. Of the more than 20 amino acids our bodies require, eight cannot be manufactured in the body. These amino acids are considered essential and must be obtained from food.

A healthy diet should include 10-15 per cent of the daily calories from protein. In practical terms, this means two to three protein servings a day. The best plant sources of protein are legumes — beans, dried peas and lentils; soya products, grains, and peanut butter. Animal foods, including milk, cheese, eggs, meat, fish, and poultry also have a high protein content.

When planning your meals, select proteins that are low in fat, such as plant products, low-fat or fat-free dairy products, fish, poultry without skin and lean meats. Avoid fatty meats, eggs and high-fat dairy products. Some situations, like pregnancy and breast-feeding, chronic illness and stress, require an extra allowance of protein.

Fats

Fats are the calorie heavyweights. They provide more than double the calories of carbohydrates and proteins, releasing nine calories of energy per gram. Though much slandered, they perform several critical functions: building the membranes that envelope the cells, producing hormones, giving insulation to the nerves, helping the body in absorption of fat-soluble vitamins, providing cushion to vital organs in the body and protecting us from extreme cold.

Chemically, fats are of three kinds: saturated, polyunsaturated and monounsaturated. Vegetable fats found in some nuts, olives, avocados, and certain vegetable oils are rich in monounsaturated and polyunsaturated fat. Cereals like wheat and rice also contain three per cent fat. The vegetable fats are more healthier than animal products, such as meat, poultry, cream, butter and lard, and many desserts and snack foods which contain saturated fats.

In the daily diet, the total fat consumption should be limited to 30 per cent or less of the total calories. Saturated fats should contribute no more than one-third of these.

Vitamins and Minerals

Vitamins and minerals are needed by the body in very small amounts. They help sustain thousands of chemical reactions inside the body. Many of these chemical reactions are linked as one triggers another. If there is a missing or deficient vitamin anywhere in this chain, this process breaks down, adversely affecting our health.

Vitamins enhance the body's use of carbohydrates, proteins, and fats. They are critical in the formation of blood cells, hormones, chemical messengers and the genetic material, deoxyribonucleic acid. In addition, beta-carotene (plant form of vitamin A), vitamin C and vitamin E also function as antioxidants, and counter the potential harm of chemicals, known as free radicals.

Minerals are inorganic elements. They play a vital role in the formation and growth of several body structures, such as teeth and bones. They also facilitate a wide range of cellular activities like muscle contraction, nerve reaction, and blood clotting.

Vitamins and minerals are found in a wide variety of foods and a well-balanced diet can fulfil the needs of the body.

Water

The human body is two-thirds water. It is a major component in the blood, lymph, cerebro-spinal fluid, synovial fluid, and soft tissues. A key player in the body's thermo-regulatory mechanism, it also maintains the natural balance between dissolved salts and water inside and outside of cells and in removing the body's wastes through urine and sweat.

You can replenish your body's water store by drinking plenty of fluids. However, those with caffeine or alcohol do not make good choice. They increase the urine output and thus dehydrate the body. Many foods are also a good source of water—fruits and vegetables, for instance, are 80 to 95 per cent water; meats are 50 per cent water; and grains, such as wheat and rice, contain 35 per cent water.

Planning your meals

A meal plan is simply a guide for eating. It helps you choose the right kind and amount of food. You can draw the plan by yourself. It is that simple. First check your weight.

Take off your shoes, step on a weighing machine, and look up straight. Once you know your height, it is easy to know where you stand!

Desirable weights for Indian men and women

Height without shoes (approximate equivalents)		Desirable weight in kilograms (ages 25 and over)	
cm	feet and inches	Men	Women
150.0	4'11"	52-56	49-53
152.5	5'0"	54-58	51-54
155.0	5'1"	55-59	52-55
157.5	5'2"	56-60	53-57
160.0	5'3"	58-62	54-59
162.5	5'4"	59-64	56-60
165.0	5'5"	61-65	58-61
167.5	5'6"	62-67	59-64
170.0	5'7"	64-69	61-65
172.5	5'8"	66-71	62-67
175.0	5'9"	68-73	64-68
177.5	5'10"	69-74	66-70
180.0	5'11"	71-76	67-72
182.5	6'0"	73-78	69-74
185.0	6'1"	75-81	71-76
187.5	6'2"	78-83	74-79

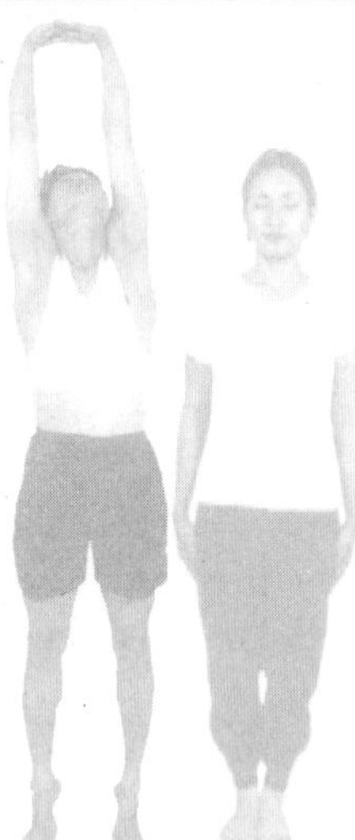

How many calories?

The daily energy requirements are guided by how much physical activity one carries out and according to one's body weight. The calculation is simple. First, locate the 'calorie factor' that applies to you:

Daily calorie requirement/kilogram body weight

How much do you weigh?	What kind of lifestyle do you lead?	
	Inactive life	***Moderate physical activity***
Overweight	25	30
Normal for height	30	35
Underweight	35	40

Now, multiply your weight by this factor to know how many calories you would need daily. Say, if you weigh 60 kg, are of normal weight and lead a deskbound life, your daily calorie allowance shall be 60 x 30= 1,800 calories. Pick an 1,800-calorie diet chart and simply follow the routine.

The food guide pyramid

If you wish to keep your daily diet plan a little more loose-ended, you could follow the food guide pyramid. The pyramid incorporates several healthy diet principles. It adds up to a plan that offers a balance of nutrients, is high in fibre and vitamins and minerals, and restricts high-fat foods. The arrangement of the food groups emphasizes the kinds of foods to eat more and those to limit.

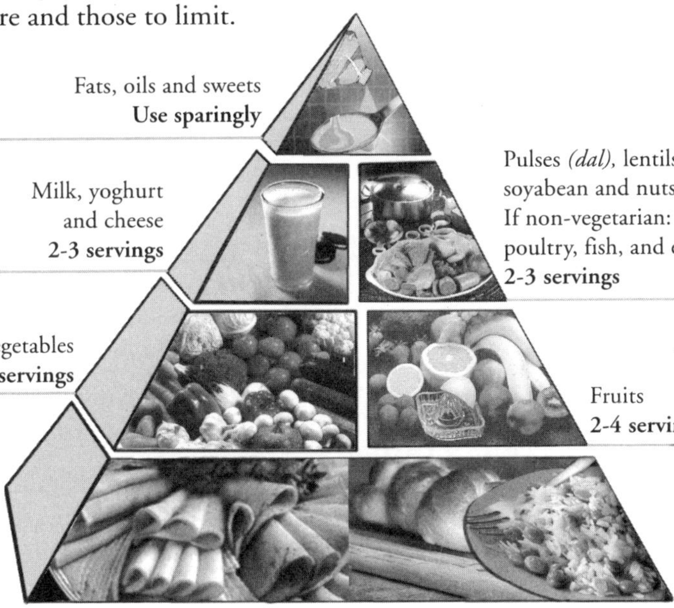

Bread, rice, and cereal: **6-11 servings**

How many servings do you need each day?

Calorie level	1,600 calories	2,200 calories	2,800 calories
Bread group	6	9	11
Vegetable group	3	4	5
Fruit group	2	3	4
Milk group	2-3	2-3	2-3
Meat group	2	2	3
Fats and oils	2 spoons	3 spoons	3 spoons
Sweets	Sparingly	Sparingly	Occasionally

Sizing up a serving

Here are some examples of what counts as one serving:

Bread, rice & cereal Group
- 1 *chapati (roti)* made of wheat flour
- ½ cup cooked rice
- 1 slice whole-wheat bread
- 1 plain *dosa*
- ¾ cup ready-to-eat cereal
- 1 *kulcha*
- 25 gram noodles

Vegetables
- 1 cup raw, leafy green vegetables
- ½ cup cooked vegetables

Milk products
- 1 cup low-fat or fat-free milk
- 1 cup low-fat or fat-free yoghurt
- 45 gram low-fat *paneer*

Fruits
- 1 apple
- 1 guava
- 1 pear
- 1 banana
- 2 oranges
- 12 grapes
- ½ cup 100 per cent fruit juice

Pulses, lentils, and soyabean
- ½ cup cooked beans, dried peas or lentils

Non-vegetarian foods
- 1 egg
- 45 gram meat
- 85 gram poultry
- 100 gram fish

Basics of healthy eating

A balanced diet contains vital nutrients fundamental to healthy living. It promotes good health, wards off disease, and allows us to perform at peak level. Taking the following steps is basic to good nutrition:

- Eat a variety of foods. It is the best way to ensure a well-balanced diet.

- Consume plenty of vegetables, fruits and grain products. They are rich in vitamins and minerals, high in fibre, low on calorie and fat, and contain natural anti-oxidants.
- Let your diet be low in fat and cholesterol. Just one tablespoon of vegetable oil per day fulfils the need of essential fatty acids. Excess fat carries too many calories, increases your weight, and puts you at risk for coronary heart disease, hypertension and diabetes. Avoid fried and junk foods; restrict butter, cream, *desi ghee*, meat, poultry, fish, and eggs.
- Avoid sweets in the diet. They add calories, and lack vitamins and minerals.
- Limit salt intake by not adding salt to foods and by eating foods that are already salted sparingly.
- Drink alcohol in moderation. If you choose to drink, drink moderately. Moderate consumption is defined as no more than two drinks per day for men and one drink per day for women.
- Just consume as many calories as essential to maintain a healthy weight.

Nutrients of life

Vitamins and Minerals

The incredible human body is much like a big busy city. It houses innumerable tiny power stations, a sophisticated communications network, unique chemical factories, an efficient transportation and garbage-disposal system, and governance that brooks no laxity. It imports several raw materials for its efficient functioning, of which vitamins and minerals are a major ingredient.

The act of putting into your mouth what the earth has grown is perhaps your most direct interaction with the earth.

Frances Moore Lappé
Diet for a Small Planet

Vitamins

Vitamins play a crucial role in the body's well being. While some vitamins are essential to the body's use of carbohydrates, protein and fats, some are vital to its growth and maintenance, and yet others participate in formation of blood cells, synthesis of nucleic acids, blood clotting factors and numerous other key processes.

Vitamins are broadly classified into two groups: fat-soluble and water-soluble. Fat-soluble vitamins are absorbed along with foods that contain fat. They can be stored in the body, and need not be consumed every day. The body stores them in fat, liver, and kidneys. In contrast, the body cannot store the water-soluble vitamins. If taken in excess, they simply get washed out in urine and therefore must be consumed every day to replenish the body's needs. The human body can manufacture vitamin D and niacin, but depends on the diet for all other vitamins. A balanced diet usually fulfils this requirement. However, if you are careless about your food habits, vitamin deficiencies can occur.

Vitamin	Food sources	Role in the human body	Deficiency/ overdose
Fat-soluble Vitamins			
Vit. A Carotene (plant source of vit. A)	Fish-liver oils, egg yolk, milk, butter Green leafy or yellow vegetables like spinach, amaranth, coriander, radish and carrot leaves, pumpkin and carrots. Fruits, e.g. mangoes, apricot, papaya, raspberry	Component of light-sensitive pigments in eye, maintenance of skin and epithelium, development of body's defence system, and essential to skeletal growth	*Deficiency:* Night blindness, permanent blindness, extremely dry skin *Excess:* Overdose may cause headache, nausea and jaundice

Vitamin	Food sources	Role in the human body	Deficiency/ overdose
Vit. D	Exists in human skin and is activated by exposure to ultraviolet light; also found in fish-liver oils, dairy products, yeast, and egg-yolk	Regulates utilization of calcium and phosphorus in bone formation	*Deficiency:* Rickets in children, bowlegs, knock-knees; in adults, softening of bones (osteomalacia) *Excess:* Kidney damage, and calcium deposits
Vit. E (Tocopherol)	Vegetable oils, peanut, wheat germ, and green leafy vegetables	Protects fatty acids and cell membranes from oxidation	*Deficiency:* Anaemia *Excess:* Ill effect on lymphocytes
Vit. K	Liver, green leafy vegetables; also synthesized by intestinal bacteria	Essential to blood clotting; role in liver production of the protein, prothrombin	*Deficiency:* Abnormally long clotting time *Excess:* Jaundice
Vit. B_1 (Thiamine)	Whole grains, yeast, legumes, nuts, organ meats, lean pork	Carbohydrate metabolism, nerve and heart function	Beriberi (weakened heart, swelling, nerve and muscle degeneration)
Vit. B_2 (Riboflavin)	Milk products, grains, legumes, liver, eggs	Synthesis of co-enzymes; biochemical oxidation and reduction	Lesions of skin, especially around the nose and lips, rawness of the tongue, mouth ulcers, and irritation in the eyes
Niacin	Wheat germ, peanuts, yeast, liver, lean meat, and fish	Component of co-enzymes in oxidation-reduction reactions in cellular respiration	Pellagra (skin inflammation, diarrhoea, and dementia)
Pantothenic acid	Milk products, egg-yolk, grains, legumes liver, and kidney	Energy metabolism	Fatigue, loss of coordination

Vitamin	Food sources	Role in the human body	Deficiency/ overdose
Water-soluble Vitamins			
Vit. B_6 (Pyridoxine)	Whole-grain cereals, milk, egg-yolk, lean meat, production of proteins, co-enzyme in carbohydrate, fat, liver, and yeast	Co-enzyme in amino acid metabolism	Decreased haemoglobin production, peripheral nerve inflammation, and convulsions
Vit. B_{12} (Cobalamin)	Liver, kidney, lean meat, fish, eggs, dairy products	Amino, fatty acid metabolism, production of proteins	Pernicious anaemia, and peripheral nerve inflammation
Biotin	Synthesized by intestinal bacteria; also found in liver, egg-yolk, yeast, kidney, vegetables, and legumes	Co-enzyme in carbohydrate, fat, and amino acid metabolism	Dry skin, anaemia, fatigue and depression
Folic acid	Whole-wheat foods, green vegetables, legumes, liver, and yeast	Synthesis of nucleic acids, rapidly synthesizing (e.g. intestinal) cells	Anaemia; maternal deficiency is associated with brain and spinal birth defects in babies
Vit. C (Ascorbic acid)	Citrus fruits, guavas, papaya, berries; vegetables such as tomatoes, peppers, cabbage and potatoes	Collagen formation in teeth, bone, and connective tissue of blood vessels; may help in resisting infection	Loss of the cementing action of collagen leads to scurvy, a condition marked by breakdown of skin, blood vessels, and gums

Minerals

Minerals are inorganic elements that are vital to the body. They facilitate healthy growth, development and maintenance of body organs and tissues and also participate in a number of bodily functions, e.g. muscle contraction, nerve reaction and blood clotting. A balanced diet provides all essential minerals, but if you do not pay sufficient attention or believe in too many diet fads, you could be in trouble.

Mineral	Food sources	Role in the human body	Deficiency/ overdose
Major Minerals			
Calcium	Milk, yoghurt, cheese, and butter; custard apple and dried apricots; raisins and dates; legumes, eggs, fish; turnip and mustard green, *ragi*, and drinking water	Essential for the formation and maintenance of strong bones and teeth. Helps to regulate the heartbeat, is necessary for blood clotting and facilitates nerve conduction	*Deficiency* Stunted growth and rickets in children, softening of bones (osteomalacia) in adults, and convulsions *Overdose* Increased calcium levels in the blood, kidney stones, impaired kidney and mental function
Chlorine	Foods containing salt; some vegetables and fruits	Maintenance of acid-base balance and fluid regulation in the body	*Deficiency* Muscle cramps, apathy, loss of appetite, acid-base imbalance in body fluids (rare)
Magnesium	Whole grains; green, leafy vegetables	Normal body metabolism	*Deficiency* Growth failure, behaviour problems, weakness, tremor, spasm, seizures, heartbeat rhythm disorders
Phosphorus	Milk, cheese, yoghurt, fish, poultry, meats, grains	Bone and teeth formation, acid-base balance maintenance	*Deficiency* Weakness, softening of bones (osteomalacia), destruction of blood cells, poor functioning of white blood cells which engulf and kill bacteria

Mineral	Food sources	Role in the human body	Deficiency/ overdose
Potassium	Bananas, cantaloupe, citrus fruits, leafy vegetables, potatoes, milk, meat	Acid-base balance and fluid balance maintenance, nerve transmission	*Deficiency* Diminished energy, muscular weakness frequent urination *Overdose* Muscle cramps, irregular heart rhythm

Mineral	Food sources	Role in the human body	Deficiency/ overdose
Sulphur	Fish, poultry, meat	Acid-base balance maintenance and liver function	Disorders unlikely
Sodium	Table salt	Acid-base balance and maintenance of water balance, normal nerve function	*Deficiency* Muscle weakness and cramps, confusion, mental apathy, reduced appetite, low blood pressure, reduced urination *Overdose* Raised blood pressure, fluid accumulation, heart failure
Trace Mineral Elements			
Copper	Drinking water, meat	Red blood cell formation	*Deficiency* Anaemia *Overdose* Deposition of copper in parts of brain, liver, and eyes causing seizures, vomiting and other symptoms

Mineral	Food sources	Role in the human body	Deficiency/ overdose
Chromium	Whole grains, legumes, organ meats, fats, vegetable oils, meat	Glucose metabolism	*Deficiency* Rise in blood glucose
Fluorine	Drinking water, tea, seafood	Maintenance of bone and teeth	*Deficiency* Tooth decay *Overdose* Mottling of teeth, skeletal handicaps, neurological disturbances
Iodine	Salt-water fish, shellfish, dairy products, vegetables, iodized salt	Essential component of thyroid hormone	*Deficiency* Enlarged thyroid (goitre) *Overdose* Depression of thyroid activity, goitre, occasional hyperthyroidism
Iron	Green leafy vegetables, legumes, whole grains especially *bajra* and *ragi*, cummin (*jeera*) seeds, coriander (*dhania*), lean meat, eggs	Haemoglobin formation in blood; formation of enzymes vital to body's energy metabolism	*Deficiency* Pallor, weakness, reduced resistance to infection, inflammation at the angles of the mouth, loss of tongue papillae *Overdose* Deposition of iron in the liver, cirrhosis
Selenium	Seafood, meat, grains	Component of an enzyme in red blood cells and other tissues	*Deficiency* Anaemia, liver injury, damage to the heart

Mineral	Food sources	Role in the human body	Deficiency/ overdose
Zinc	Seafood, shellfish, dried beans, lentils, wholegrain breads, cereals and rice, liver	Crucial to growth, development and normal function of the body. Component of many enzymes in the liver, pancreas and other organs	*Deficiency* Psoriasis like rash, eczema, growth failure, poor development of gonads, delayed puberty, slow wound healing *Overdose* Fever, nausea, diarrhoea

Cooking Practices, Food Beliefs and More

Kitchen Recipes

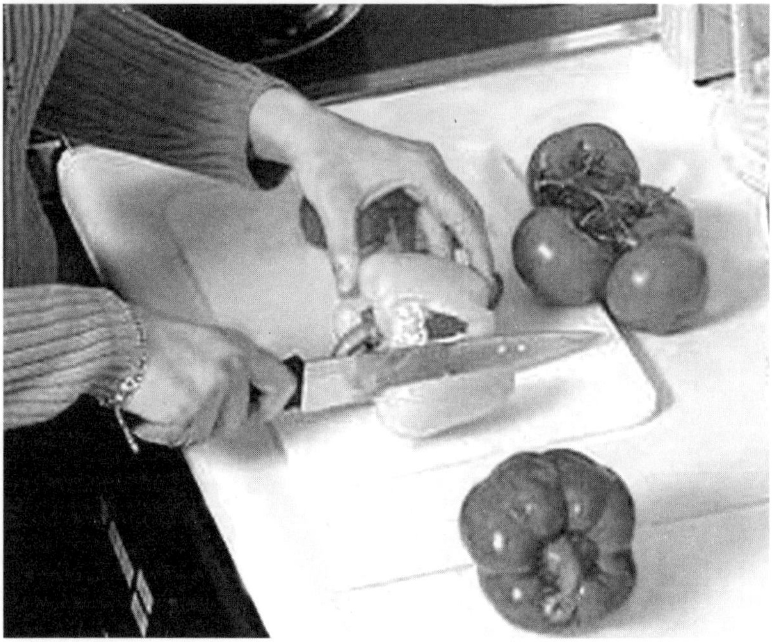

Long ago, as man evolved from his humble wilderness origins, he began to savour the warmth of glowing coals. The light of fire gave him strength over other animals and brought him into the company of other men. It was perhaps in this socio-psychological setting that he began to roast and cook food in a bid to infuse food with added energy. As time went by, he found numerous ways to process and prepare food. While these

We may live without poetry, music and art;
We may live without conscience, and live without heart;
We may live without friends; we may live without books;
But civilized man cannot live without cooks.

Owen Meredith
Lucile

---

cooking processes certainly did add to his palate-tickling delight, some left the food itself barely recognizable. Not just heat, other techniques of food preparation like simple washing, chopping, marinating and fermentation also alter the nutritive value of food in a significant way.

Even though the school of naturopathy would prefer us to return to the age of our ancestors and live on raw natural food, creative food preparation integrated with a basic understanding of the chemistry and physics of cooking can be attractive to the palate and at the same time, healthy from the nutritional standpoint.

Cut down pre-cooking nutrient loss

Several pre-cooking practices can affect the nutritive value of food. Even the seemingly innocuous practice of preliminary washing before cooking can in many cases cause a major loss of minerals and vitamins. Rice, a major component in diet in this part of the world, is one such example. Washing it with a large quantity of water can deplete as much as 40 per cent of its thiamine and niacin content. The loss does not stop here. Discarding the excess water from boiled rice before serving also leads to loss of vitamins. There is an easy way out. Use as little water as possible for washing and leave just sufficient water in the pot before cooking, so that all of it is absorbed during the cooking process.

Chopping vegetables into small pieces and leaving them on the kitchen shelf for a long time before cooking, is also not a healthy practice. The smaller the pieces and longer the time lag before a vegetable is cooked, the more is the exposure to air. This results in oxidation and loss of vitamins. The loss is most in the case of vitamin C. You could stymie this loss by introducing a few positive changes in your kitchen routine. Chop vegetables into large pieces. Never leave them on the kitchen shelf for long. Put them through the cooking process straigh away. Leaving chopped vegetable pieces soaked in water for long i one more way to lose water-soluble nutrients. They leech out int water.

Not that all pre-cooking kitchen traditions work negatively! Th routine of using sprouted foods and fermentation, such as during preparatio of *idli*, *dosa*, *dhokla*, improves both their digestibility and nutrient content The contents of vitamin C and those of the B-complex group stan remarkably enhanced.

A healthier cooking routine

When it comes to vegetables, they are best cooked on low heat i a covered vessel, using as little water as possible. This helps preserv their nutrient content, reduce cooking time and improve their flavou Excessive heating also compromises their nutritive value.

Baking soda is often added to *dals* (dried beans and lentils) t hasten the cooking process. This routine is best discarded because i leads to unnecessary loss of vitamins. Likewise, avoid boiling the mil after adding jaggery to it. This causes loss of protein and lowers th nutritive value of milk.

Some cooking practices also enhance food value. The addition o tamarind, *amchoor* and other acids at the time of cooking, a common culinar custom in Indian homes, protects against vitamin loss. Besides making foo more appealing to the palate, boiling, steaming, frying, roasting and bakin also work to destroy the potential disease-causing microbes in food. Thes processes also improve the digestibility of certain foods. For example, th digestibility and protein quality of soyabean get considerably improved o heating since it helps destroy the trypsin inhibitor—an enzyme which interfere with its protein availability. Likewise, boiling an egg eliminates avidin whic is known to bind biotin (a vitamin) and make it unavailable. Cooking als makes it easier for us to digest starchy foods.

Fruit skins and their health significance

Even though the rampant use of pesticide makes edible fruit skins a suspect, it i best to consume fruits without peelin them after a thorough wash. Rinds o apples, guavas, plums, pears and severa other fruits provide among other useful things, dietary fibre that offers several health advantages. It facilitates proper bowel function and cuts the risk of constipation, diverticular disease, and colon cancer. It also exerts a healthy influence on blood cholesterol and blood sugar level. While it helps restrict the absorption of cholesterol, it also limits the sudden spurt in blood sugar soon after a meal.

The healthier milk

Milk is a wonderful wholesome food. It is an excellent natural source of protein, fats, lactose, most vitamins, and minerals including calcium, phosphorus, sodium, potassium, magnesium, copper, iodine and cobalt, thus, making it a fine blend of the nutrients necessary for growth, development, and maintenance of the human body.

It is common belief that pure milk is far more healthier than fat-free skimmed or toned milk sold by cooperative dairy outlets, because it has more strength. There is no disputing the fact that gram for gram whole milk contains a much larger amount of fat and calories than skimmed milk; however, for most children and grownups, it is best that they take less fat and fewer calories. Saturated fats, contained in whole milk, are not very healthy and should ideally be restricted to no more than 10 per cent of the daily calories. Take a look at the nutritive value of different types of natural human and animal milk:

Nutritive value of different types of milk

(Value per 100 grams)

Nutrient	Buffalo milk	Cow milk	Goat milk	Human milk
Fat	6.5 g	4.1 g	4.5 g	3.4 g
Protein	4.3 g	3.2 g	3.3 g	1.1 g
Lactose	5.1 g	4.4 g	4.6 g	7.4 g
Calcium	210 mg	120 mg	170 mg	28 mg
Water	81 g	87 g	86.8 g	88 g
Energy	117 calories	67 calories	72 calories	65 calories

Fats and oils in cooking

Which cooking medium do you think is best? The vexing question is certainly not an easy one to answer. Over time, nutritionists have come up with different prescriptions. The present consensus is that it is best to keep all fats and oils to the minimum, and visible fats restricted to a maximum of two or three tablespoons a day. This daily allowance is best distributed equally between saturated fatty acids (SAFA), polyunsaturated fatty acids (PUFA) and monounsaturated fatty acids (MUFA).

What this translates in simpler terms is simply this:

- Use olive oil, mustard oil, or groundnut oil for their high PUFA content.
- Employ sunflower oil, safflower oil, or corn oil for their high MUFA content.
- Butter and *ghee*—if you wish to take your fill on SAFA. Palm oil and coconut oil are also high on saturated fatty acids, and therefore must be watched against.

Just so that you may understand the rationale of this exercise, here is a break up of percentage of fatty acids in common cooking mediums:

Content of fatty acids in common cooking mediums
(Percentages per 100 g)

Oil/fat	*MUFA*	*PUFA*	*SAFA*
Sunflower oil	19	69	12
Safflower oil	14	75	6
Mustard oil	59	21	12
Groundnut oil	46	32	17
Sesame oil	40	42	14
Soyabean oil	24	61	14
Cottonseed oil	18	52	26
Corn oil	28	59	13
Olive oil	74	8	14
Palm oil	40	10	50
Coconut oil	6	2	92
Butter	28	3	69

In general, the more the SAFA content of a cooking medium, the higher is the cholesterol rise associated with its use. Coconut oil is the most notorious of all. It causes a maximum rise in the unhealthy low-density lipoproteins (LDL), has a high tendency to promote fat deposition on the arterial wall and carries a high thrombogenic index, meaning thereby, that its users are at an increased risk of blood clots, coronary attacks and stroke. Hard fats like *vanaspati ghee*, hard margarine, and lard are no better.

Reuse of vegetable oils

The next time that you pour vegetable oil in a frying pan, remember to use just enough oil and if there is any left after the cooking is done, just discard it. This safety measure is necessary because fats are altered by high temperatures and turn into toxic compounds. The result is worse if the oil is used repeatedly. Vegetable oils become rancid as a result of this, picking up highly reactive oxygen that can damage the cellular components. They also polymerise, forming new harmful compounds such as peroxides, benzene and free radicals. Hydrogenation of polyunsaturated fatty acids converts them into saturated fats, making them as hazardous as *vanaspati ghee*, lard and hard margarine. They are known to raise the levels of total and LDL cholesterol and increase the rate of fat deposition in the arterial walls.

Repeated heating of food prepared in vegetable oil can be equally hazardous. The best course, therefore, is to roast, steam, grill, and bake instead of deep-frying the food.

Jamun, fenugreek seeds and blood sugar

Jamun and fenugreek seeds have for long been used as traditional cures for diabetes. There sugar-lowering utility effect has now also been validated by biochemists. Researchers have isolated an active principle, alpha glucosidase inhibitor, from the *jamun* fruit. This places *jamun* in close company with the alpha glucosidase inhibitor medication, Acarbose. Both avert the blood sugar from rising too high following a meal.

Fenugreek (*methi*) seeds also exert a blood

sugar lowering effect. They also lower the cholesterol and triglycerides. The beneficial effects of fenugreek seeds relate to their high fibre content and trigonelline, an alkaloid, to which they owe their sugar-lowering result. A daily intake of 25-50 gram fenugreek seeds divided equally and taken with morning supper and dinner (approximately two teaspoons with each meal) can be most useful for a diabetic person. The seeds can be taken after overnight soaking with water or in powder form as a drink in water or buttermilk fifteen minutes before any meal. The powder can also be mixed with flour, rice, dal or vegetables.

An expectant mother's diet

A well-balanced nutritious diet is the key to a healthy pregnancy. The belief that an expectant mother must eat for two is erroneous. The high-fat, high-calorie Indian flour recipe of *panjeeri* and *ladoos* studded with dry fruits, is certainly passé. It is best to eat moderately. High-calorie foods lead to overweight and obesity, and the extra pounds gained are always hard to shed later.

A pregnant woman needs 300 extra calories a day. She can find these extra calories in 100 ml of milk, a piece of cheese, *dal,* meat, fish and eggs, and fresh fruits and green leafy vegetables. Taking extra rations of folic acid right from the first month also makes sense. It reduces the risk of neural tube birth defects in the baby.

Additional Allowance During Pregnancy

Food item	*How much extra food you need*	*Calories*
Cereals	35 gram	118
Legumes	15 gram	52
Milk	100 gram	83
Fat	No extra allowance	—
Sugar	10 gram	40
Total		293

Source: Indian Council of Medical Research

What a nursing mother must eat?

A nursing mother must eat a well-balanced diet. It need not be elaborate. Simple *dal, roti* and *sabji,* and cheese, grilled meat, or fish, and plenty of fresh fruit make a good choice. During the first six months, a nursing mother needs 550 extra calories a day to feed the baby. This allowance drops to 400 calories, once the baby is put through the process of weaning. Feeding the baby also increases the demand on water, and the mother should drink fluids in plenty.

Additional Allowance During Lactation

Food item	*How much extra food you need*	*Calories*
Cereals	60 gram	203
Legumes	30 gram	105
Milk	100 gram	83
Fat	10 gram	90
Sugar	10 gram	40
Total		521

Source: Indian Council of Medical Research

Waxy Arithmetic

Good Cholesterol Bad Cholesterol

A wax-like fatty substance, cholesterol, wraps around each tiny cell of our little bodies. The body begins to synthesize it from the very beginning of life, and we cannot quite do without it. And yet, it holds such terror that our heart begins to race if told that its waxy arithmetic has gone wonky.

Synthesized in the body's largest chemical factory—the liver, cholesterol has several useful functions. It goes into making of the cell membranes, provides insulation cover to nerves and is an essential raw material for the production of certain hormones. The stress hormone, cortisol, and the sex hormones—oestrogen and

Gluttony is an emotional escape, a sign that something is eating us.

Peter De Vries
Comfort Me with Apples

testosterone, take shape from cholesterol. A component of the bile juice, it also helps to digest food. Clearly, cholesterol is not such a baddie; things go wrong only if we have too much of it.

More than 80 per cent of the cholesterol within us is produced by the liver. The rest comes packed in the food we eat. Foods of animal origin—milk, cream, butter, *ghee*, eggs, meat, poultry and fish contain readymade cholesterol; foods of plant origin do not. Yet, a major chunk of all excess calories, whatever their form, simply get converted into cholesterol and its partner-in-crime, triglyceride.

Just like all other nutrients, cholesterol is transported within the human body via the bloodstream. Since cholesterol is insoluble in the blood, it rides piggyback on a protein. The cholesterol-protein linkage is called a lipoprotein.

The lipoproteins are also of several kinds. They are categorized on the basis of their densities and chemical structure into low-density lipoproteins (LDL), high-density lipoproteins (HDL), and very low-density lipoproteins (VLDL). Each of them impacts our health differently, and the numbers must be watched, if you wish to keep your arteries clean.

Major forms of lipoproteins

Cholesterol carried by the lipoproteins LDL and VLDL is generally referred to as 'bad' cholesterol. It makes the arteries go bad, and has a close accomplice in triglyceride. However, one form of lipoprotein, the high-density lipoprotein, works to clean the arteries. It is therefore called the 'good' cholesterol. Let us learn a little more about how the different lipoproteins work.

Low-density lipoproteins (LDL): About 70 per cent of all cholesterol in the blood is carried by LDL particles. They transport cholesterol from its site of synthesis in the liver to the various tissues and body cells, where cholesterol is separated from the lipoprotein and is used by the cell. It is this cholesterol which is mostly responsible for the build up of fatty deposits in the blood vessels. The process is called *atherosclerosis.*

High-density lipoproteins (HDL): The high-density lipoprotein particles carry more protein than cholesterol. They scavenge or 'clean' cholesterol from the blood vessels, and transport the excess or unused cholesterol from the tissues back to the liver, where it is broken down to bile acids and is then excreted. A high HDL level is therefore associated with good health; it may actually serve to retard or reduce atherosclerotic build up.

Very low-density lipoproteins (VLDL): The very low-density lipoprotein particles are relatively large. They act as carriers to triglyceride synthesized in the liver.

Triglyceride: Chemically, triglyceride is an ester formed from glycerol and three fatty acid molecules. Fats and oils are triglycerides. In the human body, they are stored in adipose (fat) tissue or float in the bloodstream. The body synthesizes triglycerides from excess calories in foods. Excessive carbohydrates and alcohol consumption can cause triglycerides to go sky high.

Medical laboratories do a detailed work-up on the lipid profile, measuring the lipoproteins and triglyceride. It is good to remember that you must fast for at least 12 hours, before giving a blood sample for the test.

Check out: how good are your lipid numbers

Test	Healthy *mg/dl*	Borderline *mg/dl*	Unhealthy *mg/dl*
Total cholesterol	Less than 180	180-240	More than 240
LDL cholesterol	Less than 100	100-150	More than 150
Triglyceride	Less than 150	150-400	More than 400
HDL cholesterol	More than 45	35-45	Less than 35

Cholesterol and health

A skewed cholesterol or lipid profile is most damaging for the small and medium sized arteries. Once cholesterol begins to deposit on the walls, the inner diameter of the arteries gets narrowed. This reduces the flow of blood. The fat plaques also roughen the arteries, and this can lead to formation of a clot. By lodging into a narrow arterial segment, a clot can cause a sudden and complete cut off in the blood supply. If this catastrophic event occurs in any of the coronaries, it leads to a heart attack. In the brain, the same process causes cerebral stroke.

The reduction of blood flow through a narrowed artery also leads to a number of clinical conditions. The deadly coronary heart disease is the most serious. It presents as angina. Similar changes can sometimes affect the arteries in the legs, causing pain on walking or 'leg angina'. In a male, the poor blood flow can also lead to impotence.

Ways to improve the wonky numbers

If you are determined, changing the wonky lipid arithmetic to favourable numbers is not too difficult. Simple lifestyle changes—a healthier diet, reduction in weight, and regular exercise—can coast you to good health. Let us see how:

Eat to live. Watch your calories. All surplus calories are converted into cholesterol and triglycerides in the liver, pushing the unhealthy LDL up. If you wish to shed the extra pounds around your waist, then also this is a proven formula.

Stress on natural foods. Water-soluble fibre, found in whole grains, legumes, fruits, leafy vegetables, and psyllium, binds cholesterol in the intestines and promotes its excretion from the body. This helps lower the LDL, and provides the body with necessary vitamins and minerals. Natural foods rich in vitamin C, vitamin E, carotenoids, flavines and selenium, also work as antioxidants and reduce the deposition of fat in arteries.

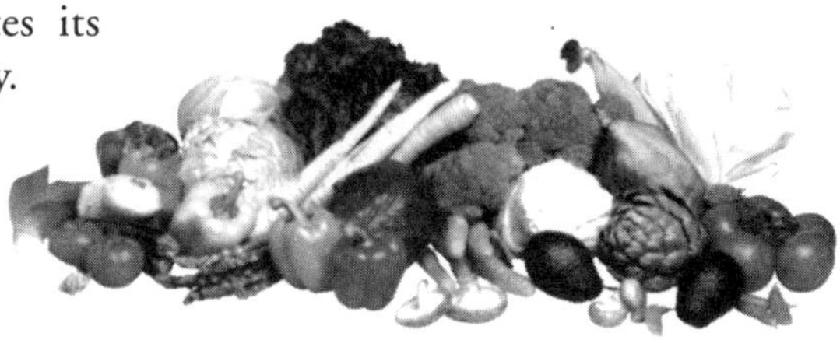

Shift to low-fat dairy products. Dairy products are high on 'hard' or saturated animal fats. Butter, scum of the milk *(malai)*, *desi ghee*, and cheese are the worst culprits. The best choice is to shift to fat-free toned milk, available at most milk cooperatives. To make a complete change, move to fat-free yoghurt and cottage cheese. Cut down on condensed milk, ice cream, cream dressings, butter and ghee.

Avoid fried foods. Deep-fried foods, such as *puri*, *paratha*, *pakoras*, *samosa*, *dalmoth*, *mathri*, *bhatura*, *cheela*, *papdi*, *vada*, *dosa*, and *uttapam* are high on calories and fat content. They may please the palate, but ruin the waistline and lipid numbers.

Junk food is bad. Pizzas, hamburgers, triple sandwiches, French fries, potato chips, cutlets and most other convenient carry-away foods are particularly bad. A single medium sized pizza has 1,400 calories, plenty of fat (the numbers depend on the toppings you choose) and very little vitamins and minerals.

Steam, bake and grill. If you like to cook, it is time to turn to a cookbook that offers recipes on how to steam, boil, grill and bake foods and still turn them into palate-ticklers.

Use healthy vegetable oils. Vegetable oils high on mono unsaturated fatty acids (MUFA) and poly unsaturated fatty acids (PUFA) make a better choice as cooking mediums. Use a mix of safflower oil, sunflower oil, wheat germ oil, corn oil, groundnut oil, and mustard oil.

Put a stop to using *vanaspati ghee*, or hydrogenated oil. It has the trans-fatty acids which increase the LDL. The worst may be coconut and palm oil.

Salads and fruits make the best snacks. If you enjoy snacking, try salads and fresh fruits. Spiced cucumber, carrots, tomatoes, lettuce, cabbage and fruits taste wonderful and are high on nutrients. In any case, *dal bhujiya*, *samosas*, bread *pakoras*, patties, cookies, pastries and cakes are prohibited.

Sugar is bad. Give your 'sugary tooth' a rest. Sweets (*mithai*), desserts, milk pudding, honey, jam, chocolates, *chutnees,* sweet potatoes, and maple sugar carry a high burden of calories.

Restrict meat, poultry and eggs. Meats, especially organ meats, sausages, lard, poultry and egg-yolk have high cholesterol content, and are therefore best eaten sparingly. Lean meats, egg-whites and poultry without skin may be the best choice.

Fish is rich. All white fish—cod, mackerel, and salmon—contain rich amounts of omega-3 polyunsaturated fatty acids. Regular fish eaters, who take 200-400 grams of white fish every week tend to have healthy HDL levels, and are at a lesser risk to develop coronary heart disease.

Use alliums. Regular intake of alliums—ginger, onion and garlic—holds several health benefits. These foods lower LDL and triglycerides, increase HDL, and reduce the clumping of platelets. They also help reduce the blood pressure. Garlic also causes dilatation of the arteries.

Restrict alcohol. Tipplers generally believe that alcohol is good for the heart, but there is clear evidence that if alcohol is to be enjoyed, it must be taken in moderation. Men must limit consumption to a maximum of two drinks per day, and women should take no more than one drink a day. Excess drinking causes an unhealthy rise in triglycerides and blood pressure, and in the long run, can cause a weakening of the heart.

Other than these dietary changes, regular exercise also pays good dividends. Just 30 to 45 minutes of aerobic exercise, like brisk walking, cycling, jogging or swimming most days of the week lowers LDL and improves the HDL fraction. Exercise also provides several other benefits: it improves the coronary circulation, adds to the respiratory reserve, lowers blood sugar, strengthens muscles and bones, reduces stress, and improves the body's immunity and well-being.

Smokers must stop smoking if they wish the HDL to rise. But sometimes, lifestyle changes do not help much. The cholesterol level may still put you at risk of a heart attack or stroke. To mend this situation, you may need medication under your doctor's guidance. Statins, a family of effective cholesterol-lowering medicines, are at hand if despite your best efforts, you are unable to bring the LDL to healthy levels. A LDL value above 190 mg/dl is reason enough to turn to your physician for advice.

Special diets for special needs

The Prescription Diet

Some diseases have a close relationship with diet. Due to the way that they are caused, some foods can play a significant role in their causation or worsen them. Several old systems of medicine, especially ayurveda, have profound tenets on this food-disease connection, but these concepts rely more on philosophical thought, rather than firm scientific facts. In comparison, modern-day biochemists, nutritionists and physicians

Eat not for material pleasure; eat to live.

Tirathankar Mahavir
Quoted in Uttara adhyan

make recommendations on definite biochemical basis.

In the following pages, a number of special diets are presented that may prove useful to you, a friend or family member.

Lactose-free diet

Lactose is milk sugar. If your body is short on lactase, a digestive enzyme found in the intestinal brush border, you cannot digest milk. The funny part is the deficiency is quite common and affects about 50 per cent people in the Indian subcontinent. If you develop abdominal discomfort, bloating, flatulence or diarrhoea following consumption of milk or a dairy food, you could be lactase-deficient. In that case, it is best to stick to a lactose-free diet and take supplemental calcium. The following foods contain lactose:

- Milk
- Dairy products
- Cheese
- Commercial bread
- Dessert mixes
- Cream biscuits
- Milk chocolate
- Creamed and dehydrated soups
- Chewing gum
- Creamed, breaded, buttered vegetables
- Commercial creamed and breaded meats
- Foods with these ingredients: milk, milk solids, dry milk, whey solids, and lactose

What to eat

To fill the void, you could take soyamilk, tofu and yoghurt. Yoghurt is usually safe since the lactose is acted upon by the lactobacillus bacteria.

Diet for ulcer and acidity

If you suffer from peptic ulcer, acidity or acid reflux, restricting certain foods can be helpful.

Some foods irritate the stomach and are best avoided. These include:

- Red and black pepper
- Coffee, including decaffeinated coffee
- Cocoa
- Alcohol
- Chilli powder
- Tea
- Cola drinks

If you have acid reflux, it makes sense to restrict foods which adversely affect the natural sphincter situated between the lower end of the food-pipe and stomach. These foods include:

- Tomatoes
- Citrus juices
- Chocolate
- Coffee
- Peppermint
- Fatty foods

In addition, it also pays dividends to change your eating pattern. Instead of three big meals, eat frequent small meals.

Gluten-free diet for celiac disease

Some people develop intolerance towards gluten—a protein found in wheat, barley, and rye. The condition is known as celiac disease. It causes inflammation in the lining of the small intestine and causes shrinkage and disappearance of its absorptive villi. Without the villi, the body cannot absorb the vitamins, minerals, and other nutrients. Over time, this causes a serious nutritional deficiency leading to a variety of symptoms: fatigue, abdominal pain, intermittent diarrhoea, bloating and flatulence.

The principal treatment is change in diet. You must stop taking those foods that contain gluten entirely. The list includes:

- Wheat flour
- White flour (*maida*)
- Wheat bran
- Wheat germ
- Wheat starch
- Barley
- Rye
- Breads
- Pasta
- Flour or cereal products
- Vegetable protein
- Malt or malt flavouring
- Vegetable gum
- Oat gum
- Vinegar
- Condiments containing vinegar

- Cereals
- Biscuits
- Cakes
- Pies
- Gravies
- Sauces
- Soya sauce or soya sauce solids
- Natural flavourings
- Caramel colouring
- Brown rice syrup
- Vanilla
- Alcohol

Sometimes you may find gluten in objects that you would never expect. For example, if you were to use a knife for spreading butter that has breadcrumbs on it or eat deep-fried foods cooked in the oil that has been used previously to fry gluten-containing foods, you could be courting trouble. Lipstick, postage stamps, and medication pills or tablets can also contain gluten.

What can you eat?

The list of gluten-containing foods is so long that you may wander what foods would be safe for you to eat. If you think deep, the situation is not that bad. You could eat rice, legumes, dairy products, vegetables, potatoes, fruits and plain meats.

Foods and migraine

Some foods and beverages can also initiate a splitting headache. The attack occurs due to vascular disturbance initiated by one or the other chemical constituent in the food. The best form of prevention lies in identifying the possible head busters and shying away from them. Take a check:

- Chinese cuisine (with monosodium glutamate)
- Oranges
- Ripe bananas
- Vinegar
- Yeast
- Processed cheese
- Chocolate
- Tinned foods (which contain sodium nitrite/nitrates)
- Red meat
- Sherry and red wine

Low salt diet

If you suffer from high blood pressure, a failing heart, chronic kidney failure or accumulation of fluid in the body, you may need to limit the sodium intake in your diet. This may help reduce the blood pressure and the tendency to retain fluids. Limiting sodium may also help your heart to work more effectively.

Processed foods are the worst culprits. Salted snacks, convenience foods, pickles, and sauce contain especially high amounts of salt (sodium chloride). If you wish to go on a sodium-controlled diet, avoid or limit the following foods:

- Table salt
- Pickles, olives
- Chutneys
- Sauces, especially soya sauce, mustard sauce and tomato ketchup
- *Namkeen bhujiya, dalmoth, mathri*
- *Chat-pakori,* French fries, and fast food
- Potato chips and popcorn
- Cow's milk
- Processed cheese
- Salted butter and peanut butter
- Salted crackers and biscuits
- Pastries, cakes, and ice-creams
- Salted nuts
- Canned foods (except fruit)
- Amaranth, *litchi*, and melon
- Cured meats
- Sausages, ham, bacon
- Sea fish
- Commercial salad dressings
- Instant cooked cereals
- Frozen foods
- Antacids

Coronary heart disease prevention diet

Keeping the body's serum cholesterol low is one way to keep your coronary circulation in good health. Diet can play a major role in this. A healthy diet can reduce your risk of coronary heart disease by a good one-quarter.

Fruits and Vegetables

- Eat plenty of fresh fruits and vegetables. If the fruit skin is edible, you may as well consume it.
- Eat potatoes, sweet potatoes and parsnips in moderation.

Cereals

- Eat wholemeal flour, wholegrain bread, wholegrain cereals, oats, wholegrain rice, legumes and sprouted gram.
- Restrict white flour (*maida*) preparations, such as bread, *kulcha* and *nan*.

Dairy products

- Take skimmed milk, low fat cheese, yoghurt, and curd.
- Pass up full cream milk, condensed milk, cream, full-fat cheese.

Eggs and Meat

- You may take up to 200 gm of meat, preferably rabbit and poultry.

- Lean meat, liver, and kidney can also be eaten in moderation.
- Take no more than two whole eggs per week.
- Avoid visible fat in meat, pork, duck, fried meat, sausages and burgers.

Fish

- Eat white fish (cod, mackerel, salmon); 200-400 gm of oily fish per week is ideal.
- Avoid fried fish.

Fats and Oils

- Keep all fats and oils to the minimum; limit visible fats to 20 gm/day.
- Use olive, safflower, sunflower, sesame, cottonseed, corn, and groundnut oil in moderation.
- Keep away from hard fats like *vanaspati*, butter, *ghee*, palm oil, coconut oil, regular cheese, margarine and lard.

Cakes and Desserts

- You may eat low-fat puddings, *kheer* and *jalebi*.
- Restrict cakes and desserts.
- Avoid *khoya* sweets, dairy ice-cream, and chocolates.

Salt

- Use minimum salt.

Diabetic diet

Contrary to popular thought, having diabetes does not mean that you have to follow a highly detailed diet plan. For most people, having diabetes simply translates into variety and moderation — eating more of certain foods, such as grains, legumes, fruits, and vegetables that are high in nutrients and low in fat and calories, and less of others, such as sweets, junk food, processed foods, and animal foods. There is also a need to bring in discipline. It would be best if you were to eat at the same time, about the same amount of food, and the same proportion of carbohydrates, proteins and fats. This will help keep your blood sugar at a steady level. It is more difficult to control your blood sugar if you eat a big supper one day and a small one the next. Also, the more food you eat at one time, the higher your blood sugar will rise. Eating at regularly spaced intervals — meals spaced four to five hours apart — reduces large fluctuations in blood sugar and also allows for adequate digestion of food.

You should avoid foods that provide calories but no nutrients. The list includes:

- Sugar, glucose, jam, marmalade, honey, syrup, treacle, tinned fruits, sweets, chocolate, lemonade, glucose drinks, proprietary milk preparations and similar foods which are sweetened with sugar
- Cakes, sweet biscuits, chocolate biscuits, pies, puddings, thick sauces
- Jam, marmalades, and tinned foods
- Alcoholic drinks

Low-purine diet for gout

A low-purine diet is advisable for people who suffer from gout, high uric acid content in the body or uric acid stones in the kidney. It can help lower the uric acid in the body by up to 10 per cent. The following foods increase uric acid in the body:

- Spinach, cauliflower, peas and beans
- Mushrooms
- Whole pulses (*saboot dals*)
- Dried beans (*chana*, *rajma* and *lobia*)
- Lentils (*masur ki dal*)
- Organ meats: liver, kidney, sweetbreads (pancreas of calves), meat extracts, poultry, ham, and sausages
- Seawater fish including sardines, shrimp, mackerel
- Alcoholic beverages
- Tea, coffee and cola drinks

At the same time take a low-calorie low-fat diet, and reduce your weight. Uric acid rises if a person is overweight or obese. It is also a good idea to maintain good hydration. Drink lots of water, at least ten to twelve glasses a day. This will help flush the uric acid crystals out of your body.

Low oxalate diet

A low-oxalate diet is useful if you have had an oxalate kidney stone before. It shall lower your risk of recurrence. The following foods have high oxalate content and are best avoided:

- Black gram
- Spinach
- Almonds
- Cashewnuts

- Amaranth
- Mustard green
- Curry leaves
- Drumstick leaves
- Mustard leaves
- Gogu (*pitwa* or *ambadi*)
- Lotus stem
- *Amla*, *phalsa*, strawberries and plums
- Rhubarb
- Red chilli
- Chocolate
- Cocoa
- Tea

High fibre diet

A high-fibre diet offers several benefits. It keeps you free from constipation, irritable bowel, diverticulosis and colon cancer; it reduces cholesterol, improves the control over blood sugar, and reduces the risk of heart disease. As a general rule, take more fruits and vegetables, leaving the skin on, whenever possible, and avoid processed food. Also, take your pick from the following foods:

The very high-fibre foods

- Peas and red beans (*lobia*)
- Psyllium husk (*isabgol)*
- Wheat bran, cornflakes
- Almonds
- Dried apricots, figs and prunes

The high-fibre foods

- Spinach and baked beans
- Whole meal flour/whole wheat bread
- Groundnuts
- Raspberries, black currants and blackberries
- Dates and raisins

The medium-fibre foods

- French beans, carrots, cabbage, beetroot and sweet corn
- Lentils and sprouts
- Apples, bananas, pears, plums and strawberries
- Walnuts

Common Adulterants and Contaminants

The Safety Factor

The safety and nutrient value of the foods we consume is jeopardized by a number of adulterants and pesticides. It is a marvel that the human body can take so much abuse. The adulterants can be in any form and hard to recognize. While some may just chip a tooth, leave you with a bad mouth, or abrade the stomach, others are so toxic that they can damage the kidneys, liver, spleen, lungs, skin, nervous system, testis and ovaries and lead to anaemia, organ damage, nerve injury, paralysis and cancers. No food is quite safe, and manufacturers and merchants fear no ethics in compromising the health of the consumers. Unless a larger consumer movement

My art and profession is to live.

Michel de Montaigne
Essays, "Of Exercise or Practice"

or moral change sweeps our present social structure, individual safety lies in being mindful of the risk, and buying foods at quality conscious food stores.

The adulteration practices are so numerous and variable that it is hard to detail them here; however, a list of common adulterants and their ill effects on the human body are presented.

Toxins and adulterants in foodgrains

The safety of grains, beans and lentils may get compromised at the time the crop is raised, stored or just before it is sold to the consumer. The impurities can range from relatively innocuous sand particles, marble chips and pebbles to talc, saw dust, asbestos, and toxins which can lame or kill a person.

Foodgrains	Adulterant/Toxin	Possible ill effects
Legumes *(dals): arhar, masoor, chana* Bengal gram flour (*besan)*	*Lathyrus sativus* (*Kesari dal*), a cheap crop, is mixed with the gram or flour. It contains the toxin, beta oxalyl amino alanine.	Neurolathyrism, a crippling disease. It affects mainly men in the age of 15-45 years. At first, it causes ungainly gait, but, if neglected, it paralyses both the legs.
Wheat, rice, maize, groundnut, and cotton-seed	Fungi *A. flavus* and *A. parasiticus*, which infest foodgrains due to poor storage conditions, and release aflatoxins.	Toxic to liver, and can cause cirrhosis. Can also lead to cancer.

Foodgrains	Adulterant/Toxin	Ill effects
Wheat, *bajra*, rye, and sorghum	Ergot fungus, which grows on the crop and causes a blackish disfigurement of the harvested seeds	Ergot poisoning. Acute effects include nausea, repeated vomiting, giddiness and drowsiness. Chronic effects include painful cramps and gangrene of the limbs
Wheat, rice, maize, dried peas, beans and lentils	Marble chips and pebbles	Chipping of tooth and damage to the lining of the alimentary tract
Wheat flour, white flour (*maida*), arrow-root powder	Talc, sand particles, and sub-microscopic fibres of asbestos	Cancer of the stomach and gastro-intestinal tract

Adulterants in edible oils

Edible oils and fats are also subject to adulteration. Oils extracted from naturally growing harmful crops, industrial chemicals, used automobile oils, and cheaper edible oils are mixed with widely used edible oils. They can cause serious harm to the health of the consumer.

Edible oils	Adulterant/Toxin	Ill effects
Mustard oil Groundnut oil	Argemone oil extracted from prickly poppy is mixed with edible oils. The oil contains a toxic alkaloid, sanguinarine, which interferes with the oxidation of pyruvic acid and leads to its accumulation	Epidemic dropsy marked by sudden swelling in legs, diarrhoea, breathlessness, heart failure and death. Some people develop glaucoma
Vegetable oils	Industrial solvent, orthotricresyl phosphate (TCP)	Permanent damage of the myelin nerve sheaths, causing paralysis and sometimes death
Vegetable oils	Mineral oil, petroleum fractions including used automobile oil, and paraffin oil. They may also contain polycyclic aromatic hydro-carbons, which are toxic to the human body	Vomiting, diarrhoea, and interference with absorption of fat-soluble vitamins. Polycyclic aromatic hydrocarbons are also carcinogenic (cancer-causing substances)

Adulteration of dairy products

Adulteration of milk has been practised for so long that the dishonesty of *doodhwalas* is a legend. The simplest adulterant is water, but starch, synthetic milk and various other agents are mixed with equal aplomb.

Adulterant	Ill effects
Addition of water, which may be contaminated and may carry disease-causing microbes	Water-borne diseases like typhoid, cholera, and shigellosis, if the milk is taken without boiling. Loss of nutritional value
Extraction of fat and addition of starch (arrowroot flour, white flour, etc.) to make milk more viscous and to increase its density	Loss of nutritional value
Synthetic milk (a combination of urea, sodium chloride, sodium bicarbonate, sucrose, vegetable oil, detergent and water)	No nutritional value. Can prove toxic

Adulteration of condiments

Spices are much a part of the Indian cuisine. They are also used for seasoning of foods. A variety of adulterants are often mixed with them for petty pecuniary benefits. Some of these can be toxic to the body.

Food articles	Common adulterants
Dhania powder	Starch, cowdung, horsedung powder
Chilli powder	Sawdust, brick powder
Asafoetida (*hing*)	Sand particles, resins, gum
Turmeric (*haldi*) powder	Sawdust, chalk powder, toxic colours
Black pepper	Dried papaya seeds
Cumin (*jeera*) seeds	Grass seeds coloured with charcoal dust, and spurious cumin seeds prepared from soil mix
Cardamom (*eliachi*)	Removal of oil and lacing pods with talc
Cinnamon (*dalcheeni*)	Cassia bark
Cloves (*luang*)	Removal of essential oil
Saffron (*kesar*)	Dyed tendrils of maize cob
Betelnut (supari)	Coloured sawdust
Tea	Dried, powdered, artificially coloured leaves, coloured sawdust, black gram husk
Coffee powder	Date husk, tamarind husk, chicory

Toxic colouring agents

Various foods, from the mouth-watering confectionaries, ice-creams, *boondi ka laddoo, jalebi, Karachi halwa* to button mushrooms, candies, jams and juices, fresh green peas and cheese burgers may owe their bright inviting colours to toxic colouring agents. These can cause serious ill effects ranging from birth defects, anaemia, kidney damage, liver injury, and hydrocephalus to mental retardation, impotence, tumours, and cancers.

Food articles	Toxic agent	Colour	Ill effects
Ice lollies (*barf ka gola*), sweets (*mithai*), jams and juices, asafoetida, saffron, and yellow dried beans	Metanil yellow	Yellow	Degeneration of testes in men
Fresh green peas, chilli powder, *churan*, jams and juices	Malchite green Rhodamine B Blue VRS Sudan III	Green Red Blue Red	Congenital malformation of eyes, bones, skin and lungs. Increased risk of tumours of the lungs, liver, breast and ovaries
Sugar coated *saunf*, and betelnut *Karachi halwa*	Auramine Orange II	Orange Orange	Kidney and liver damage
Asafoetida (*hing*)	Lead chromate	Yellow	Anaemia, abortion, mental retardation
Spices, jams, juices, and tinned foods	Congo red	Brownish-red	Serious birth abnormalities: hydrocephalus, hydronephrosis and eye defects

Pesticides and foods

Pesticides are chemicals designed to kill, control, or repel insects, mites, nematodes, rodents, weeds, and fungi. They are to protect used standing crops and in storehouses where the harvest is stocked. A recent ICMR study found that contamination with pesticides is common in India. While more than 50 percent samples showed some contamination, 20 percent samples had pesticide residues, in excess of maximum tolerance limit. They carry serious health risks and can cause birth defects, damage the peripheral nerves, spinal cord, and brain, induce liver injury, lead to infertility and impotence, suppress the immune system and spark leukaemia, sarcomas, lymphomas and cancers.

Ill Effects of the Commonly Used Pesticides

Pesticides	Ill effects
Acephate	Toxic effect on the reproductive tract; may induce genetic mutation and cancer
Aldicab Carbofuran Methomyl Phorate Profenofos Quinalphos Triazophos	Each is a cholinesterase inhibitor and can result in a variety of symptoms including weakness, blurred vision, headache, nausea, sweating, and tremors
Aldrin	Lung cancer, chronic liver damage
Butachlor	Weight loss, reduction in brain size
Captafol Captan Cypermethrin Fenthion Parathion	Can cause mutations in cells, and possibly cancer
Carbaryl	Can cause mutations in cells; damage the kidneys and nervous system; produces N-nitrocarbaryl—a carcinogen—in stomach; can cause non-Hodgkin's lymphoma
Carbendazim	Disrupts the production of sperms and affects testicular development; also may damage a developing embryo
Chlordane	Toxic effects on the reproductive tract, blood disorders, non-Hodgkin's lymphoma, and brain cancer
Chlorpyrifos	Chronic neuro-behavioural effects like persistent headache, blurred vision, unusual fatigue, muscle weakness, and problems with mental function including memory and concentration lapse, irritability, and depression
DDT	Chronic liver damage causing chronic hepatitis and cirrhosis, endocrine and reproductive disorders, polyneuritis, immuno suppression, breast cancer, and non-Hodgkin's lymphoma
Diazinon	Non-Hodgkin's lymphoma

Pesticides	Ill effects
Dieldrin	Liver damage, Parkinson's disease and Alzheimer's disease
Dimethoate	May be toxic to the reproductive tract, and cause birth defects and cancer
Deltamethrin	Endocrine disrupter
Endosulfan	Effects kidneys, liver and testes adversely, lowers semen quality, causes immuno-suppression, promotes testicular, prostatic and breast cancer, and may cause birth defects in a developing foetus
Ethion	Impaired memory and concentration, disorientation, severe depression, irritability, confusion, headache, speech difficulties, delayed reaction times, nightmares, sleepwalking, and drowsiness or insomnia
Fenitrothion	Retinal degeneration, frontal lobe impairment, and neurological deficits
Fenvalerate	Reduction in weight
Heptachlor	Reproductive tract abnormalities, blood disorders
Isoproturon	Tumour promoter
Lindane	Allergic dermatitis, chronic liver damage causing chronic hepatitis and cirrhosis, polyneuritis, endocrine and reproductive disorders, breast cancer, non-Hodgkin's lymphoma
Malathion	Carcinogenic, has been linked with leukaemia; chronic health effects include: allergic reactions, delayed neuro toxicity, behavioural effects, damage to eyes, abnormal brainwaves and suppression of immune system; may cause mutations and birth defects
Mancoze	Ethylene thiourea, a product of mancozeb metabolism, can cause goitre; also possibly birth defects and cancer
Monocrotofos	Can cause delayed neuropathy
Paraquat	Parkinson's disease and Alzheimer's disease
Permethrin	Genetic damage, cancer potential, and neurotoxic effect on growing foetus
Simazine	Cancer of testes
Trifluralin	Prolonged or repeated skin contact can cause allergic dermatitis, decreased red blood cell counts, and increased methemoglobin, triglycerides, and cholesterol